# The Truth About Creation & Evolution

## More Than 75 Ways Science Supports Creation and Disproves Evolution

## Robert Knopf

An O.M.N.I Publication
Woodland, Washington
creationproof.com

Thanks to Dr. Kent Hovind, Dr. Dennis Swift, Pastor Glenn Morrisey, and to Dick, Nancy and Becky Knopf for reviewing the manuscript. Particular thanks to Dr. Kent Hovind whose inspiration led to the writing of this book.

Design by Christine Beneda

ISBN 0-9671346-3-3
Library of Congress Catalog Card Number: 2005911301

Published by:
Outdoor Management Network Inc. (O.M.N.I. Publishing)
4607 NE Cedar Creek Road
Woodland, Washington 98674

First Edition
Published in the United States of America

All Biblical references are from the King James Version of the Holy Bible

Web site: http://www.creationproof.com
Email: omni@creationproof.com

**Attention Churches, Universities, Libraries and Schools:**
Quantity discounts are available on bulk purchases of this book for educational, gift purposes, or use as premiums. Special books or book excerpts can also be created to fit specific needs. For information, please contact: Creation Science Network, 4607 NE Cedar Creek Rd., Woodland, WA 98674, or phone 360-225-5000.

# TABLE OF CONTENTS

# The Truth About Creation and Evolution

Creationist Viewpoint: *"In the beginning God created the heaven and the earth"* (Genesis 1:1).

Evolutionist Viewpoint: *In the beginning the heavens and earth created themselves from nothing.*

**Evolution and creation are both religions.**

# CHAPTER 1

# Brainwashed
# By Evolution

## Evolutionary Theory

It can be difficult to identify exactly what evolutionists believe because evolutionary theory has changed frequently over the years, and different people would describe evolution differently.

Generally, evolutionists claim that 18-22 billion years ago all the matter of the universe was concentrated into a compressed dot smaller than the size of the period at the end of this sentence. This "dot" blew apart forming primordial earth, the planets, the solar systems and galaxies. This is called the "Big Bang" theory. Then, supposedly, 4.5 billion years ago, primitive earth, a molten rock spinning through space, began to cool. Water vapor condensed causing rain, which washed the rocks and formed the oceans. According to evolutionary theory, about 3.5 billion years ago, in the oceans, untold "billions" of substances accumulated, a few of which came together into "living assemblies." These living assemblies, termed primordial slime, evolved into today's plants and animals and eventually into man, the most elevated animal form.

Believing this is like believing that a pencil, given enough time, will evolve into a pen, a book, a radio, a TV, a bicycle, a car and eventually into the space shuttle. Evolution is preposterous by any measure, and evolutionists can't answer even the most basic questions, such as: Where did space (the universe), time and matter originate? How could the universe, stars, planets and solar systems evolve from nothing? How could all the matter in the universe become squished into something smaller than the period at the end of a sentence? How can life begin spontaneously from nothing?

## Kinds of Evolution

There are six broad categories of evolution.

**Cosmic evolution** is the origin of time, space, and matter from nothing, called the "Big Bang" theory.

**Chemical evolution** is the evolution of all elements and chemical substances from primordial hydrogen.

**Stellar and planetary evolution** is the evolution of the earth, galaxies and solar systems from cosmic dust particles.

**Organic evolution** is the evolution of non-living matter into living organisms by spontaneous generation.

**Macroevolution** is the evolution of a single living cell into today's complex array of plants and animals, including mankind.

Each of these types of evolution theorizes that what we see today came from nothing through unknown, unrecorded, un-measurable and unproven processes. This belief, by definition, is unscientific, illogical and impossible to prove. We cannot identify how it happened. We can't simulate or replicate it. We can't measure it. It is not science; it's a religion, an un-provable belief.

**Microevolution** or **Variation,** the sixth type of evolution, is the natural (and man induced) variation that occurs when a plant or animal kind produces a variation of itself. Evolutionists sell evolution by citing variation. Variation is observable, repeatable and real. Thus it is scientific. This is the process by which horses, dogs, cats, roses, corn and other species develop into different varieties of the same kind. However, hundreds, thousands or millions of years of variation does not become evolution. A variety of dog will never become a cat. A variety of rose will never become corn or wheat.

Evolutionists claim that today's plants and animals, including man, are the result of gradual change beginning with a "simple" living molecule. Over billions of years this molecule supposedly evolved into bacteria, protozoa, fish, reptiles, birds, mammals, and eventually man. This "molecules to man" theory is the core of evolutionary belief, the core of their religion.

To help sell evolution to the public, evolutionists use extreme amounts of time. This is their attempt to make the unbelievable seem believable. Just like a fairy tale: "Millions of years ago and far, far away…" Since we can't picture millions or billions of years, the claim of "millions of years" attempts to make the impossible seem possible, the unbelievable seem believable. These long periods of time are conjecture based on faulty assumptions. Evolutionary theory is comprised of fraudulent and pseudo-scientific evidence, based on the assumption that God doesn't exist and didn't create the world.

## An "Evolution" Example:

Let's pretend that, as you and I walk across a dirt and gravel parking lot, we look down and find a digital cell phone lying on the ground. Obviously, we know the cell phone had a designer, even though it is much less sophisticated than a living cell. Let's say that I'm an evolutionist. I pick up the cell phone and say, "Look what evolved from gravel and rock over millions and millions of years." If I actually said this, you'd think I was a nutcase because just like the evolution of man, this observation defies all logic since we can see inherent design in the phone, the same way we can see the inherent, miraculous design in the human body.

You make the argument that cell phones weren't invented until the late 1900's, so the phone couldn't be millions of years old. You then continue, "Digital cell phones weren't invented until around 1990, and email and Internet models weren't available until around 2000." Plus, you continue, "Up until an hour ago, it has rained steadily for the last three days, and the phone isn't wet or rusty. Plus, the phone is turned on and the batteries are fully charged." By this time, most people would agree from the actual evidence that the cell phone didn't evolve from dirt and gravel but that someone dropped it quite recently. They accept it had a designer even though the designer can't be seen. Each individual fact fully disproves the cell phone evolved from dirt and gravel. However, as an evolutionist, one who doesn't believe in an intelligent designer, I later publish a book, *"Origin of the Cell Phone…"* on my theory about how the cell phone evolved, disregarding all evidence to the contrary.

> *"Often a cold shudder has run through me and I have asked myself whether I may have devoted myself to a fantasy"* (Charles Darwin *Life and Letters*, 1887).

This is similar to how evolutionists such as Darwin and others ignored and continue to ignore scientific facts. In addition, some have even created fraudulent evidence to keep evolutionary theory alive. It only takes one factual piece of evidence to prove a cell phone didn't evolve from dirt. Likewise, it only takes one factual piece of evidence to show man didn't evolve from primordial slime.

## Brainwashed By Evolution

Most people believe in evolution because it is all they've ever been taught and because it has been labeled as "science." They've been duped. The average person, including the average scientist and student of science, has been taught since prekindergarten that the earth is billions of years old and that mankind evolved from an ape. School textbooks continue to print evolutionary theories (stated as fact) even though the foundations of these theories have long ago been proven false. The truth is that evolution is the greatest fraud in (scientific) history. No one has proven evolution and no one can. The scientific facts corroborate creation.

Many scientists actually believe in creation; however, they cannot voice scientific or mathematical viewpoints for creation without being ridiculed by their peers. Also, many people and organizations have a direct atheistic, political or monetary agenda, and endorse evolution to further their agenda. To believe in evolution, scientific laws must be broken or twisted like a pretzel. Those who believe in evolution have been mislead, lied to and cheated from the truth. They have indeed been brainwashed.

## Evolution Is A Religion

Evolution is the party line of atheists, and has given us socialism, Marxism, Stalinism, Communism, Nazism and humanistic doctrines that throughout history have thrown mankind into war, persecution and racial prejudice.

Evolution's founding premise is that the earth, the universe and life itself created themselves from nothing. A Christian's founding premise is that God exists and God created space, time and matter, the universe and life. Both evolution and Christianity are religions.

Christians believe, "In the beginning God created the heaven and the earth." Evolutionists believe, "In the beginning heaven and earth created themselves from nothing." Evolutionists offer no plausible explanation for how space, time and matter came into existence, who made the laws of science, or what supplied the original energy needed to form the universe.

Atheistic evolutionists like Hutton, Lyell, Darwin, Stalin, Marx and Hitler developed and promoted the evolutionary theory. Adolf Hitler once said, "Tell a lie big enough, loud enough, and often enough and people will believe it." Hitler also said, "Let me control the textbooks and I will control the state." This is happening today in our schools and universities as students are brainwashed to believe in evolution. Since the evolutionist's mindset is that God doesn't exist, evolution is their ridiculous attempt to explain what God did, without God.

## Nothing Can Create Itself

The main problem with evolution is that if God didn't create the world, the world had to create itself from nothing. Inherently, this is absurd. Anyone will quickly realize that for something to create itself, it would first have to exist. If it exists, it has already been created.

Life from nothing is termed spontaneous generation. Louis Pasteur disproved this in the late 1800's. Even with today's technology, life has never been created in a laboratory from non-living chemicals, even though thousands of scientists have spent their lives trying. If we cannot bring a dead animal or person back to life, when the exact components that make up the liv-

Cavemen didn't exist. They were either ape or man. Artistic renderings that show a half ape, half man, are artistic conjecture unsupported by either bone findings or fossil evidence.

ing animal or person are present, how can anyone believe life began by accident, when the components for life didn't exist?

## Simple Questions Evolutionists Can't Answer

The test of any scientific theory is whether it answers simple, basic questions. Many well meaning though mis-guided people think evolution is a reasonable theory that answers man's questions about the universe. However, there are hundreds of basic questions evolutionists can't answer. Here's a sampling.

Where did the space for the universe come from?

Where did original matter come from?

Where did time come from?

How did thought begin?

Where did the laws of the universe come from?

How did matter get so perfectly organized?

Where, when and how did life arise from non-living matter?

Where, when, and how did life learn to reproduce?

Why would an animal reproduce, since this causes competition for resources?

How can mutations (evolution) of a genetic code produce a new species with completely different DNA?

How can mutations in the genetic code add to the genetic code?

How did "evolved" species survive when they were half fish, half reptile, or half reptile, half bird?

Why aren't any valid intermediate forms found in the fossil record?

Why aren't there living intermediate stages today where one animal is evolving into another?

How would a fish know it would be better to live on land?

Cannot everything in evolutionary theory be better answered by creation?

Although evolutionary concepts cannot answer or explain these questions (although they will try), each is perfectly explained by creation. Creation is detailed in the Bible, our most accurate and best-preserved historical record. The biblical account of creation is also fully backed by science.

*The biblical account of creation
is fully backed by science.*

# CHAPTER 2

# *The Creation Story*

## The Truth

Creationists believe in an all-knowing, perfect God who created and controls the universe and all that exists. The creation story is fully detailed in the Holy Bible, the greatest historical record of all time. Many don't realize it, but science fully supports the biblical account of creation.

## The Creation Story

Approximately 6,000 years ago, God created the heavens and earth, man, plants and animals, the stars and the galaxies. God did it in six days in a very specific order. He first created time, space (the universe) and matter. He formed the heavens and the earth. He divided the earth into dry land and the seas. He created the sun, moon, stars solar systems and galaxies. He created plants, fish, birds and both sea and land mammals. He created man and woman to govern the earth and all that is on it. He created all this in six days and declared the seventh day holy, a day of rest. This gives us our current seven-day week.

The scientific record tells us the original earth was quite different than today. It was perfect. There were fewer and smaller seas so man and animals could travel from continent to continent worldwide. There was a protective atmospheric layer of water vapor, a hydrosphere, surrounding the earth. This created a "greenhouse" effect and perfect climate. It protected man and animals so they could live forever. There was more oxygen then, so man would heal quickly, run faster, have more endurance. Plants and animals would grow larger. God specifically created the earth to be inhabited, to be perfect.

Earth was warm and tropical, and inhabitable from pole to pole. There were no deserts, no towering mountains, and no polar ice caps. The fossil record shows many plants and animals were larger then. There are fossils of 60-foot tall cattails, beavers eight-feet long, huge insects, birds, mammals and, of course, dinosaurs. Man was possibly bigger too and skeletal remains show that some men were giants, up to 12 feet tall. Contrary to evolutionists' claims, dinosaurs lived with man, and because of the warm climate, lush (huge) plant growth, and higher oxygen levels, dinosaurs thrived. Dinosaurs, called dragons in those days, grew quite large, up to 100 tons and 60 feet tall, but some were as small as a chicken. Most dinosaurs were the size of a horse.

> *The scientific record tells us the original earth was quite different. It was perfect.*

This all changed when man (Adam) chose to disobey God. God's judgment came upon man, the land, plants and animals, and all that lived on the earth. In these times, man did evil continuously, which displeased God.

Because of this, God advised Noah that he would cause a flood to cover the total earth, killing all life on land. He instructed Noah to build an ark, a large floating ship. Noah was to take two animals (a male and female) for each kind of animal on earth onto the ark to save them from extinction. The ark was huge, at least 450 feet long, 150 feet wide and 45 feet high. It had three decks and could hold an estimated 16,000 animals and all the needed food and provisions. It was equivalent in size to 522 railroad cars.

Noah took two of every animal, male and female, and seven pairs of bird kinds and select animals, such as goats, sheep and rams. He took dinosaurs too. Obviously, he'd take younger specimens of these larger animals to conserve space.

After Noah and the others had entered the ark, about 4,400 years ago, God caused a great, worldwide flood to destroy all mankind and all land animals except those on the ark. This flood and associated cataclysmic activity shaped the world we see today.

To create a worldwide flood, God caused the earth to open up, and water burst forth from large underground rivers and caverns. At the same time, God caused it to rain for 40 days and 40 nights without stop. The hydrosphere (water layer) that surrounded the earth emptied its contents. Since there were no tall mountains then, water covered the total surface of the earth and everything on earth drowned except Noah, his wife, his three sons, their wives (8 people total), plus the animals on the ark.

When God created the earth, he created different "kinds" of plants and animals. Over time (4,400 years since the worldwide flood) these initial kinds of plants and animals diversified through variation into the many plants and animals of today. Today, there are more than 250 varieties of dogs, but they are all dogs. Today, there are hundreds of varieties of corn, but all of them are corn. One kind of plant or animal cannot "evolve" into a more advanced or different kind as evolutionists speculate. They can only diversify into a similar kind.

Thus, Noah only took different "kinds" of animals onto the ark: a pair of dogs, a pair of cats, a pair of horses, etc.

## God's Word: The Holy Bible

True science, history and archeology support the writings found in the Bible, the oldest and best documented book in the world.

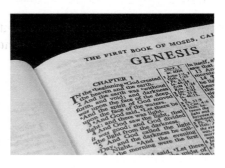

Although the Bible was completed about 1500 years ago, it contains hundreds of prophetic statements and hundreds of scientific insights not understood by scientists until modern times. It is a true and accurate account of earth history. The Bible is God's Word to mankind, written by 40+ men over a period of 1600 years. Since God knows exactly what He did at creation, the Bible is a perfectly true record of creation and early mankind. The Bible is meant to be taken exactly as it is written, without being molded or changed to fit man's erroneous views on evolution.

It's clear from the Bible that we did not evolve from primordial slime. Even today, scientists can't find one single credible example where one kind of animal evolved into another, or became more developed or more advanced due to natural selection or mutation. If evolution were true, there should be billions of intermediate animals and intermediate anatomical systems, but none are found either alive today or in the fossil record. If evolution were true, the more "primitive" forms of life, plants and all lower animals would be continuing to evolve today, and we should see living intermediate forms. This just isn't happening. In truth, God created the heavens and the earth and all that is in them. He created specific kinds of animals, fully formed and fully functioning since their creation.

> *If evolution were true, the more "primitive" forms of life, plants and lower animals would be continuing to evolve today, and we should see living intermediate forms. This just isn't happening.*

# CHAPTER 3

# *Two Opposing World Views*

A person's belief in either creation or evolution results in huge differences in their individual viewpoint of the world. Creation is God-focused. Evolution is an anti-God deception. These views are polar opposites. When looking at the four great philosophical questions concerning mankind, our answers are based on our belief in either creation or evolution. This belief structures how we view the world and the scientific record.

## Four World View Questions

### *Question #1:* **Who am I?**

**Evolutionists believe:** We are descendants from primordial slime. We're animals. We have no obligation to anything or anyone. There are no rules of right or wrong, no moral code, except what man makes or chooses. Man is god.

**Christians believe:** We were made by God and are God's servants. God is the boss. God gave us rules (laws, commandments) of right and wrong by which to live. We are responsible for our actions.

### *Question #2:* **Where did I come from?**

**Evolutionists believe:** Man came from primordial slime that formed billions of years ago. Man originated as an accident, a mistake, a mutation, and evolved by random chance from a single-celled bacterium.

**Christians believe:** God created mankind (man and woman) in God's image about 6,000 years ago. We are descendants of Adam and later Noah. We were created perfectly by God, and only through sin did death and human degradation begin.

### Question #3: Why am I here?

**Evolutionists believe:** Man has no purpose except to have a happy life where anything goes. If it feels good, do it. Why not? We are accountable only to ourselves. We make the rules. There are no absolutes. We are in charge.

**Christians believe:** We have responsibilities to God and man. We will be held accountable for our actions. We are servants and owe service to God and man. We should follow God's rules.

### Question #4: Where am I going when I die?

**Evolutionists believe:** When you die, it's over. You die forever, so enjoy life while you can.

**Christians believe:** When we die, we will be judged by Jesus Christ. Christians will spend eternity in heaven with God. Our afterlife will be greater, more wonderful than we can imagine. Those not in a relationship with God will spend eternity with Satan in the Lake of Fire.

Our belief system is controlled by whether we believe in evolution or creation. Our world beliefs set the framework for how we deal with others and ourselves. Belief in either creation or evolution is incompatible with belief in the other. Those who believe in both have been duped. They typically believe that "God controlled evolution," called theistic evolution. This false belief has no basis in science or in Scripture. It implies that God isn't capable of creation without billions of years of evolution, including suffering and death, to help things along. Theistic evolution is unscientific, unscriptural and impossible when we examine the scientific facts.

*Our belief in either evolution or creation determines our total behavior system.*

# CHAPTER 4

# *Evolution Spawned Human Persecution and Racial Prejudice*

## The 1700's

To understand evolution, we must take a peek at history. In the late 1700's, the Bible dramatically influenced people. At this time, James Hutton, a devout atheist, wrote the book, *Theory of the Earth*, which claimed (without scientific proof) that the earth was "millions of years old." This began the theory of Uniformitarianism. This theory states, "The present is the key to the past" and that our world was formed gradually over a huge period of time.

## The 1800's

Then, in 1830, Sir Charles Lyell, a lawyer, who hated religion and ridiculed the Bible, wrote: *Principles of Geology*. This book is the "bible" for geologists. Lyell stated (without facts) that the earth is "billions of years old," and he developed a "geologic (stratigraphic) column." This column doesn't exist except in textbooks. It is a model, which uses fossils and earth layers to show a "historic" past. Each rock layer was given a name and an age, e.g. Cretaceous Layer (Age), etc. He claimed each layer was identified by an "index fossil," a fossil that supposedly indicates the age of the rock layer in which it is found. The rock layers date the fossils. The fossils date the rock layers. This is circular reasoning.

The earth does have rock layers, and it does have a fossil record, but these were formed quite rapidly during and immediately following the worldwide flood about 4,400 years ago. However, kids are taught about the geologic column and evolution from preschool through college, and endless repetition throughout schooling causes them to disbelieve the Bible and the fact that God created the heavens and earth.

## Racism Influences

Charles Darwin read Lyell's book. Then, when studying finches on the Galapagos Islands, he noticed different beak varieties (variation). In 1859, he wrote the book: *The Origin of the Species.* The full title is: *On the Origin of Species by means of Natural Selection, or the preservation of <u>favored races</u> in the struggle of life.* Darwin took variation (which is real) and invented macroevolution without any evidence. He stated (wrongly) that all living things had a common ancestor.

---

*Evolution promotes racism.*
*Creation teaches all men and women*
*are created equal.*

---

In truth, Darwin was a racist. This was a time when slavery and persecution of blacks prevailed. He disliked blacks and ridiculed women. Evolution justified racism and was an attempt to show that white men (according to Darwin) were farther evolved than blacks, Jews, or Orientals. Darwin also felt women were inferior, and Darwin's writings are speckled with statements that blacks, Jews, and women were inferior and had diminished brain capacity. Obviously this is not true; however, evolution has been a major contributor to worldwide racial prejudice. Creation, on the other hand, teaches that all men and women are created equal.

### Darwin Quotes:

*"To suppose that the eye ... could have been formed by natural selection, seems, I freely confess, absurd in the highest degree"* (Charles Darwin, *The Origin of Species by means of Natural Selection or the preservation of favored races in the struggle for life).*

*"A married man is a poor slave, worse than a Negro"* (Charles Darwin, *The Autobiography of Charles Darwin).*

*"Whether requiring deep thought, reason, or imagination, or merely the use of the senses and hands ... the average of mental power in man must be above that of women"* **(Charles Darwin, Descent of Man).**

## The Ism's

Evolution and its associated racism created other "isms." Evolution spawned: Uniformitarianism, Marxism, Stalinism, Nazism, Communism, Humanism, and Socialism. Belief in evolution was instrumental in the mass murder of so called "inferior races" - Jews by Hitler and Poles by Stalin, among others. Hundreds of Australian Aborigines were killed because they were thought to be the missing link between "caveman" and modern man.

In U.S. history, we mistreated Native Americans because of an evolutionary mindset. We called them "savages" – and unjustly labeled them an "inferior genetic race." This is another negative influence of evolution.

## Outright Fraud

In 1860, Earnst Haeckel read Darwin's book and he saw there were no intermediate life forms where one kind of plant or animal evolved into another. There were no intermediate fossils between a salamander and a lizard, or a fish, bird, and mammal. So, to help the "cause," Haeckel fabricated "proof." He made fake drawings of embryo development for different groups of animals showing

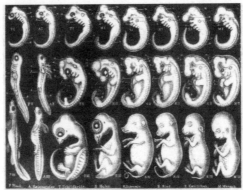

Haeckel's infamous drawings purporting to show embryos in development as published in Germany, 1874.

**Haeckel's Fake Drawings, 1874**

Haeckel's fake embryo drawings still appear in textbooks today. Why? If all the fraud and untruths were taken out of school textbooks, nothing would remain to support evolution.

## Haeckel's Fake Drawings on Top

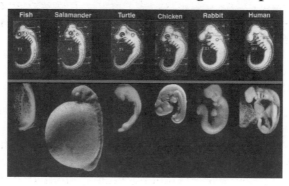

## Actual Embryo Photos on Bottom

fraudulent similarities. His drawings do not match the way the embryos actually look and he was convicted of fraud in 1874 at University of Jena where he did his schooling (his alma mater). However, his drawings are still found in school textbooks today, even though they were proven false more than 100 years ago.

## Persecution of Man

Adolf Hitler believed in Darwin's evolutionary theory. Because of evolution, Hitler believed that Germans were a superior race. According to Hitler, not all people were people. Aryan was the prime race, then Norwegian, German and Slavic. According to Hitler, Slavics were thought to be half man, half ape. Orientals were mostly ape; black's were mostly ape. Jews were the lowest race based on Darwin's evolution, and Hitler called them pure ape. According to Hitler, Jews were a parasite, not a people. In 1936, the German Supreme Court ruled that Jews were not people. They used evolution to discredit life and to justify killing innocent Jews.

Joseph Stalin believed in evolution. He read Darwin's book, *Origin of the Species*, and killed an estimated sixty to one hundred million Ukraines. He took their crops, starving them to death. He justified this because in his eyes they were a less evolved race. He also used his belief in evolution to execute 14,700 Polish officers because Poles were declared "sub-human."

Karl Marx, the Father of Communism, dedicated his book, *Communist Manifesto*, to Charles Darwin. Marx, an evolutionist, still negatively influences millions today with his racist teachings.

The truth is that there is only one race, the human race, and all men and women are created equal – by God.

## Abortion

Although we are appalled at Hitler's persecution of the Jews, the U.S. has done similarly. In 1973, the U.S. Supreme Court ruled that an unborn child (called a fetus to dehumanize it) was not a person and was not protected by the 14th Amendment (the right to life). The Supreme Court ruled that life begins at birth, which anyone inherently knows is not true. Life begins at conception. However, to allow "a women's right to choose" (to choose death for an infant), U.S. courts determined, like the German court, that not all people are people. So today, we continue to kill unborn babies every day. At this writing, there have been an estimated 49 million babies aborted in the U.S. alone, and an estimated one billion worldwide. There have been more deaths by abortion in the U.S. than all U.S. military deaths in all U.S. wars.

## In Summary

Hutton's book, *Theory of the Earth,* caused people to doubt God's creation and tried to explain an old earth. Lyell's book, *Principles of Geology,* tried to explain the world without a flood and presented the geologic column. Darwin's book, *Origin of the Species,* tried to explain away God as creator.

The truth is that scientific, historical and archeological evidence shows that about 6,000 years ago God created mankind, the earth, the universe, and all that was created. About 4,400 years ago a worldwide flood and associated cataclysmic activity shaped the world we know today and formed all the geologic layers in the days, weeks and months following the flood.

Section II will provide more than 75 proofs for a young earth, including that cavemen did not exist, that dinosaurs lived with man, and that God created heavens, earth and mankind.

# CHAPTER 5

# Six Key Factors Disprove Evolution

Believers in evolution must not only disregard logic, they must ignore hundreds of known scientific facts, including several scientific laws. However, six major problems show evolution isn't possible.

## #1: First Law of Thermodynamics Disproves Evolution

The First Law of Thermodynamics states that matter can neither be created nor destroyed. Evolutionists throw out this law. If God didn't create the world, the world had to create itself. To create itself, it would already have to exist. If it exists, it can't create itself. Absurdities like this are why creation was removed from school textbooks. If evolution and creation, each a religion by definition, are compared side-by-side, the fallacy of evolution would be clearly seen.

## #2: Second Law of Thermodynamics Disproves Evolution

The Second Law of Thermodynamics states that all matter and energy in a closed system moves from a state of order to a state of disorder or randomness. This includes the planets and the universe. The earth, solar systems and galaxies are winding down, becoming more random. This is exactly opposite the theory of evolution, which says that things are becoming more ordered, more advanced and more complex. Evolutionists must throw out the Second Law of Thermodynamics. There is not one credible example of a living group of organisms, or organ system evolving from less complex, such as a molecule, to more complex, such as forming a human, a human brain, or an eye. Each plant and animal we have today was created (designed) for a specific purpose.

## #3: The Law of Conservation of Angular Momentum Disproves Evolution

The Law of Conservation of Angular Momentum sounds difficult to understand, but it merely means that fragments or pieces that come off a spinning object will spin in the same rotational direction as the object. If, as proponents of the Big Bang claim, a spinning dot created the galaxies, solar systems, planets and stars, all planets, galaxies and solar systems would spin in the same direction. They don't. In our own solar system, Venus and Uranus spin in opposite directions. Plus, some entire galaxies spin in opposite directions. These facts alone disprove the Big Bang Theory as explained in most modern day textbooks.

# #4: Spontaneous Generation Can't Happen

Spontaneous generation is a false belief that life comes from dead or non-living matter. Louis Pasteur disproved this in the late 1800's. To believe in evolution, you must believe in spontaneous generation. Life from non-living material has never been observed and is impossible to create even in a laboratory. We've never come close to simulating how minerals from rock and water could possibly become energized to become alive. Evolutionists use "billions of years" to try to overcome the absurd assumption that life can arise from non-living matter, but at some specific instant dead matter would have to come to life. The truth is that regardless of how many years you tack onto this process, non-living matter will not become alive.

# #5: Reproduction Disproves Evolution

If we assume that life created itself (which it didn't), how did it learn to reproduce? Were two similar "entities" created at the exact same time in the exact same place? Why would something want to reproduce? This would give competition to itself and defies the concept of survival of the fittest. How would any primitive "entity" know how to make itself better, or even what "better" would be? Why would a fish think it would be a good thing to crawl out on land, when it hadn't seen land? How would a moral conscience develop since this is contrary to self-interest and survival?

# #6: No Scientific Evidence Supports Evolution

The truly major problem with evolution is that there is no scientific evidence to support it, only conjecture, imagination and fraud. It is a highly flawed theory at best. Evolution is simply man's attempt to explain how earth and mankind got here without God.

# Science Supports Creation

A reasonably accurate way to tell the age of something is by using "chronological clocks." These "clocks" use current observable and ongoing changes that, when viewed backwards in time, help identify the true age of man, earth and the universe. There are many such clocks. They indicate God-creation, and that the earth, man and the universe are only a few thousand years old.

# CHAPTER 6

# Not All "Science" is Science

The world of science is complex. Scientists generally do an excellent job of understanding ongoing processes when they can test and replicate actual occurrences through experimentation. However, they have done a terrible job of formulating ideas about how earth and man originated because from the start they rule out creation by an intelligent designer. They throw out objective scientific analysis to support their preconceived idea of evolution. Their religion, evolution, gets in the way of true understanding.

Scientific findings that support creation become "filtered," twisted and distorted to match evolutionary theory. Data that doesn't match evolutionary theory is thrown out. Special interest groups, whose mission is to keep God out of public domain, or those who seek monetary research grants, attack any scientific discovery that even implies God made the heavens and earth.

In the last hundred years a few scientists have even perpetrated hoaxes, disguised as science, to promote the evolutionary theory. Some of these hoaxes remain in textbooks, in museum displays and are seen daily on TV "documentaries." They continue to brainwash an unknowing public.

For example, man didn't evolve from an ape, and cavemen never existed. Skeletal and fossil finds are either true man or true ape. Early man was more perfect than we are today. However, this isn't what evolutionists portray. You can read volumes about how apes evolved into man, but when you examine the objective evidence, there is none. It is important to mention that graphic artists make the half man, half ape drawings we see in textbooks without any evidence to support these drawings. They are fabrications.

A good example is Piltdown Man, a supposed primitive man (a missing link between ape and man). Piltdown Man was a hoax. The skull of a man was fitted with an ape jawbone by filing them so they fit together. They were treated with acid to age them and the fabricated skull was buried and later "re-discovered." For decades, however, Piltdown Man was reported as fact in school and college textbooks.

Nebraska Man was another supposed link between ape and man. He was fabricated from the finding of a single tooth. From this one tooth, drawings were made showing a half man, half ape-like creature, and a complete story of Nebraska Man was fabricated, presented to the public, and taught for years in public schools. Later, it was determined that the tooth was actually from a pig.

Nebraska man was actually a pig.

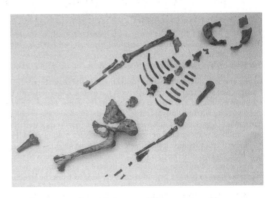

The current missing link for modern man is called "Lucy." Here again graphic artists have taken great liberties to construct a half human, half ape-like being. Although Lucy has given us a more complete skeleton than most supposed transitional forms of man, the things that actually separate man from ape, such as the greater portion of the skull, the knees and the ankle bones are missing from the skeletal finds of Lucy. Artistic drawings, however, give Lucy human-like feet and stature, but this is pure conjecture. In reality, Lucy is an ape.

Scientists have developed radiocarbon and other dating techniques based on equally erroneous assumptions that support their "billions of years" theory about the age of the earth. Today, school textbook authors keep perpetuating old, outdated, and erroneous theories, many proven wrong more than 100 years ago. Our children continue to be brainwashed at school, by TV, and in children's books that continue to claim our ancestry evolved from an ape. This is science fiction not science. This has also had dire consequences on our youth. If you tell kids they are animals, they will act like animals.

Throughout history, "science" has been wrong many times. The theory that bleeding cures disease contributed to the death of George Washington. The theory that heavy objects fall faster than light ones lasted hundreds of years until Sir Isaac Newton proved this wrong. The list of "science" errors goes on, in seemingly endless fashion.

The following chapters present true scientific findings in thumbnail fashion compiled from hundreds of published scientific papers. Many of the items listed are "chronological clocks." These "clocks" use current observable and measurable events that can be extrapolated backwards in time to determine the age of man, the earth and the universe. Contrary to evolutionary theory these clocks show a young earth and prove that man, the earth and the universe were created at the same time.

The following facts also show that evolutionary theory is impossible. As you review these, it is important to remember that like the cell phone story, in many instances, just one fact, by itself, proves evolution isn't possible. For example, to believe in evolution you must believe that the universe, earth, and man made themselves from nothing – a philosophical and scientific impossibility.

Since, in this short publication we cannot list the hundreds of scientific references used to compile these examples, those interested should visit www.creationproof.com, which provides links where anyone (believer or skeptic) can view the true scientific record. Also listed at the end of this book are publications and sources where references to the original scientific documentation can be found.

# CHAPTER 7

# Earth Evidence Supports Creation

### Geological evidence shows a young (approx. 6,000 year old) earth

**Background.** There is solid scientific evidence to show the earth is not billions of years old. Science also shows that earth is uniquely positioned among the planets to support life. Earth has exactly the right amount of oxygen, nitrogen and water. It has hot and cold temperature cycles conducive to life. The features that make life possible on earth cannot be explained by mere chance or by evolution. Our earth's ability to hold life can only be explained by a Master Designer – God. He specifically designed the earth to be inhabited.

Current evolutionary theory is based upon James Hutton's misguided theory of Uniformitarianism introduced in the late 1700's. Its basic assumption is that earth's geological features developed by gradual change over billions of years. His claim was that the present is the key to the past. However, using modern day "clocks" we see the earth can only be a few thousand years old.

The truth is that approximately 6,000 years ago, God created the heavens and earth, mankind, animals, plants and all that was created in six days. About 4,400 years ago, a worldwide flood shaped the earth we know today, and formed the various geological layers. During the flood, rains poured from the sky and subterranean water chambers, "fountains of the deep," broke open spewing out hot, volcanic water. These events killed animals and plants and covered the entire earth's surface with water. Due to the yearlong flood with extreme tidal fluctuations, sediment movement and associated tectonic activity, the soft soil layers bent and uplifted. Caverns that held underground water collapsed. Geological formations such as the Rocky Mountains, Himalayas, and Grand Canyon uplifted and formed in days, weeks and months as the earth underwent the most extreme cataclysmic transformation in history. Following are other facts that show the fallacy of evolution.

**Earth's Spin.** The earth spins on its axis at a speed of 1000 mph at the equator. The earth's spin is slowing down by 1/1000 second each day. If the earth were billions of years old, it would have spun so fast initially, we would have all been slung into space. There would have been instantaneous day and night occurring every few seconds. Winds would have been 5,000 mph. Obviously, this wasn't the case.

**Geological (Rock) Layers.** Geologists often refer to a hypothetical geological column that uses fossils to identify the date of the geological rock strata, and uses the rock strata to date the fossils. This is circular reasoning. Geologic layers were not laid down over millions of years, but were formed by hydrologic sorting due to extreme tidal surges on earth during the yearlong, worldwide flood 4,400 years ago. As further proof, many geological rock layers show bending, indicating the rock was soft (from the flood) as the layers quickly formed.

**Rock Layer Erosion.** If each earth layer were millions of years old, you'd expect erosion from weather and rain between the various rock layers. However, only the top layer shows erosion. There's no erosion between the different rock layers, indicating they were laid down quickly.

**Meteor Dust.** Meteors strike the earth constantly, creating meteor dust. Each of the earth's geologic layers, which supposedly represent millions of years, should have meteorites in them.

They don't. Only the top layer has meteorites. The other layers were created fast (during the flood) and only the top exposed layer has existed long enough to have meteorites in it.

**Grand Canyon.** When looking at the Grand Canyon, an evolutionist would say, "Look what happened in millions of years." A creationist would say, "Look what the worldwide flood did in days and weeks." In actuality, the river basin

at the entrance of the Grand Canyon is lower than the top of the canyon. The river couldn't have carved the canyon. The Grand Canyon was created by the release of waters as the earth buckled following the worldwide flood. In 1980, the Mt. St. Helens eruption produced similar geological canyons along the Toutle River. They developed in the days and weeks immediately following the eruption, not over millions of years.

**Rocky Mountains and Mt. Everest.** The Rocky Mountains and Mt. Everest formed during and following the flood. The tops of the major mountain chains worldwide have trillions of fossilized clams - and clams don't climb very well. The clamshells are closed indicating they died quickly as sediment developed around them. They also indicate that the land that now makes up Mt. Everest and the major mountain chains were once underwater.

**Mountain Ranges.** Mountain ranges often follow the seacoast. This is because the mountains lifted up and the seas sank down as the earth buckled during and following the worldwide flood.

**Oldest Tree.** The oldest tree in the world, a California Bristlecone Pine, is dated at 4,300-4,500 years old. Why is there not an older tree? The reason is that all trees were killed in the worldwide flood approximately 4,400 years ago.

## Land Erosion.

Yearly erosion of mountains and landmasses indicates the earth is only a few thousand years old. At today's soil erosion rates, the tallest mountains would have eroded completely flat (to sea level) in 14 million

The Brisletcone Pine, approximately 4,400 years old, is the oldest living tree. Why not an older tree? Because the worldwide flood killed them 4,400 years ago.

years. They would have eroded flat five times since evolutionists claim dinosaurs roamed the earth. Erosion would have also destroyed all the geological layers and fossils, and would have flattened all the earth's geological features.

## Sedimentation.
At today's sedimentation rates there is only enough ocean sediment for the earth to be several thousand years old. If the earth were billions of years old, there should be significantly more sediment.

## Mississippi River Delta.
The Mississippi River deposits an average 80,000 tons of mud/hour at its delta. The delta grows larger each day. If this mud was deposited uniformly over time, the sedimentation found represents about 5,000 years of deposition. If the earth were millions of years old, the Mississippi River delta would extend to Africa.

## Niagara Falls.
Erosion has caused Niagara Falls to move 4.7 feet a year backwards (until 1930 when water was diverted and erosion lessened). It has moved a total of seven miles. If the earth was billions of years old, Niagara Falls should have moved hundreds of miles. If we assume that Niagara Falls water flow was

constant over time, the distance it moved represents 9,900 years of movement. However, extremely high flows following the worldwide flood caused much of the erosion in weeks and months. The actual age of Niagara Falls is 4,400 years of normal flow, plus the torrential flow following the worldwide flood.

**Underground Caverns.** Stalagmites and stalactites have

been reported to take 250 million years to form, growing one inch in 1000 years. Not true. There are already 15-inch stalactites under the Lincoln Memorial, built in 1922. An abandoned coal mine 55 years old has huge stalactites more than 10 feet long.

**Oil.** Underground oil is often found at pressures of 20,000 psi (the reason for oil gushers). The pressure is held there by the surrounding rock. Oil experts say the oil pressure would have leaked off and there would be no pressure in only 5-10,000 years. The truth is that oil was created from the massive quantity of dead matter (plants and animals) killed in the worldwide flood. It remains under pressure today because modern earth is only about 4,400 years old.

**Coal.** Geologists claim it took "billions of years" to form coal and that it happened long before man. But coal has been found to contain human artifacts (gold chain, shoe sole). Coal formed much more recently and quickly.

**Ice Cores.** Ice core samples from the arctic show the earth is less than 5,000 years old. What were once thought to be "annual" rings in the ice have been shown to be simply periods of heating and cooling. Measuring actual ice development over the last 50 years has shown that the ice formation on the poles has only been occurring for about 4,000 years.

**Lost Squadron.** In WWII the Lost Squadron landed P-38 planes in Greenland out of gas. In 1990, 48 years later, 263 feet of ice covered the planes. Ice was deposited at 5.5 feet per year. Measuring the thickness of arctic ice and using this rate, gives 4,400 years of ice at the arctic, the amount of time since the worldwide flood.

**Sahara Desert.** Prevailing winds cause the Sahara Desert to grow 3-5 miles larger each year. It is only 1,300 miles across. This indicates it has only been a few thousands years since the desert began forming.

**Earth's Magnetic Field & Carbon Dating.** The earth's magnetic field, a barrier that protects us from UV radiation is weakening, decreasing by half every 1400 years. This is okay if the earth is only 6,000 years old. However, because of this, life would not have been possible even 10,000 years ago. There is only a few thousand years left before magnetic field weakens so that all life on earth will die off. (We're already seeing more "ray" bombardment today). The magnetic field indicates the earth is young. The weakening electromagnetic field also introduces significant error into carbon dating methods, which erroneously assumes a constant magnetic field. Carbon dating methods, thought by laymen to be highly accurate, are fraught with errors based on incorrect assumptions.

**The Earth Itself.** Even with thousands of scientists trying to show life on other planets, only one planet in our solar system and beyond has been found suitable for life – Earth. It is perfectly and uniquely positioned to allow life, defying all statistical probability. The Bible (Isaiah 45:18) states, *God formed the earth to be inhabited.* No other known planet comes even close to having conditions that would support life.

# CHAPTER 8

# The Universe Supports Creation

### Our solar system and the universe were created in six days, not in billions of years.

**Background.** Evolutionists claim a dot, containing all the matter in the universe exploded in a "Big Bang." This supposedly created the solar systems, stars and galaxies we have today. In actuality, the universe was created by the hand of God. He supernaturally created the heavens and the earth, mankind, plants and animals in six days.

**Planet Rotation.** The Law of Conservation of Angular Momentum disproves the Big Bang theory. If, as evolutionists claim, a spinning dot of matter exploded in a Big Bang, all planets and fragments would also spin and orbit in the same direction. This is the Law of Conservation of Angular Momentum. However, some moons, plus the planets Venus and Uranus, spin in opposite directions. Many planetary moons not only spin backwards, they orbit backwards. Some entire galaxies revolve backwards. These facts alone disprove the Big Bang theory.

**Shrinking Sun.** The sun is slowly losing both mass and diameter each year. Every hour it shrinks about two feet or .4% each thousand years. If the earth is 6,000 years old, the sun has shrunk approximately 2.4%, not a problem. However, if the earth were 5 billion years old, the sun initially would have been double its present diameter. More 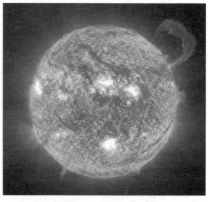 importantly, 30 million years ago the surface of the sun would have touched the earth. Life couldn't have existed on earth even one million years ago. It would have been too hot.

**Moon.** The moon orbits around the earth, and is drifting two inches farther away from earth each year. It is only 240,000 miles from earth. The moon causes the earth's tides. If the earth and moon were billions of years old, initially the moon would have been so close to the earth that extreme tides would have drowned all life. More realistically, however, the moon would have been pulled into the earth by the earth's gravity.

**Cosmic Dust.** Cosmic dust lands on earth and washes into the ocean. It has high nickel content. If cosmic dust was deposited uniformly over time, there is only enough cosmic dust in the oceans to represent earth's existence for 18,000 years. In actuality, it represents 4,400 years of erosion, plus extreme runoff following the worldwide flood.

**Moon Dust.** Outer space is full of dust. Plus, the moon has no wind. Scientists calculated one inch of

Man's footprints on the moon show only ½-1 inch of moon dust, indicating the moon is only about 6,000 years old.

space dust would fall on the moon every 10,000 years. They concluded there could have been as much as 54 feet of space dust covering the moon surface. The feet of the Lunar Lander had saucers and extender rods with sensors to study the deep sediment they thought the Lander would sink into. However, there was only one half to one inch of dust. Why was there so little dust? The solar system, moon and earth are only about 6,000 years old.

**Saturn's Rings.** Saturn's rings are moving out, getting farther away from Saturn. Saturn can't be billions of years old or its rings would be completely gone by now.

**Planet Cooling.** Planets are still cooling off. Jupiter and Saturn have not yet reached thermal equilibrium. If the planets were billions of years old, they would already be fully cooled (at equilibrium).

**Stars.** We've never seen a star form. The star Sirius was reported 2,000 years ago as a red giant star; today it's a white dwarf. It only took 2,000 years to cool this amount, not the billions of years scientists claim. Stars are going the opposite direction of evolution: cooling, and not being created. Scientists have never observed a new star being formed. Why? Because God created them all at the same time.

**Spiral-Shaped Universe.** The elliptical shape of our universe should be randomized (have no shape) in billions of years. However, it still has an elliptical shape, which it gradually continues to lose, showing it's only a few thousand years old.

**Comets.** There are several hundred comets in our solar system, significantly less than the number reported in Greek and Roman times. Comets disintegrate over time and have short lives. They should all be gone (burned up) in less than 10,000 years. Since they still exist, this shows the galaxies are less than 10,000 year old. To counter this, and to support their religion, evolutionists fantasize that there is a comet "nest" (Oort cloud) that keeps making new comets, even though this has never been observed nor shown.

# CHAPTER 9

# Mt. St. Helens Evidence Supports Creation

### Mt. St. Helens disproves Uniformitarianism and the geological ages.

**Background.**
The 1980 Mt. St. Helens eruption shows in miniature how many of today's geological features were formed. The eruption and related ash and water slides

and flooding in 1980 created the same pattern of geological layers found elsewhere in the world that scientist's claim took millions of years to form. These geological features formed in hours, days and weeks following the 1980 Mt. St. Helen's eruption.

**Juvenile Water.** When volcanoes erupt much of the eruption matter is water. Since this is new water from deep underground, it is called juvenile water. Each year the earth's volcanoes contribute one cubic mile of new juvenile water. There are 340 million cubic miles of water in the oceans. If the oceans began with no water (they didn't), it would only take 340 million years to fill today's oceans. Actually, God created the oceans 6,000 years ago.

**Canyon Formation.** Great erosion ditches at Mt. St. Helens formed similarly to the Grand Canyon. These happened in hours and days, not millions of years. The sides of carved canyons show layering just like the Grand Canyon. The Toutle River flows through the Toutle Canyon, but normal river flow didn't create the canyon. Molten rock, water and ash from a debris dam breaking, coupled with snowmelt from the eruption created the canyons. In other areas of the world, catastrophic events of the worldwide flood created formations like the Himalayan Mountains, the Grand Canyon and the Dakota Badlands.

**Geologic Layers.** At Mt. St. Helens, layered soil and rock formed in weeks as ash and water runoff formed into rock layers. Many soil layers are bent because they were soft as they formed, just as we find in other places in the world.

**Polystrata Forests.** The Mt. St. Helens eruption blew thousands of trees into Spirit Lake creating 2,000 acres of floating and sinking wood. Vertical trees now extend (upright and upside down) through deposited ash layers on the lake bottom. These exactly resemble Polystrata forests found in numerous places around the world, which geologists claim took millions of years to form.

# CHAPTER 10

# Ocean Evidence Supports Creation

**Background.** Our oceans are getting larger as polar ice caps melt, not due to global warming, but to natural processes. The "salt" content of the oceans is caused by minerals from land eroding into the seas.

**Mineral Runoff.** At earth's beginning the seas and oceans may have been freshwater. The oceans continue to get saltier today due to mineral runoff. Today, they have 3.6% salt (mineral) content. If the earth were billions of years old, the oceans would have more minerals and would be significantly saltier.

**Ocean Floor Sediment.** Sedimentation of the ocean floor is only a few inches deep. If the earth was billions of years old ocean floor sediment would be many feet deep. Ocean sediment depth indicates the earth is only a few thousand years old.

**Great Barrier Reef.** The Great Barrier Reef in Australia, the world's oldest reef, has been determined to be about 4,200 years old. Why isn't there an older reef? Because modern earth was shaped during the worldwide flood and related cataclysmic activity 4,400 years ago.

The Great Barrier Reef is approximately 4,200 years old. Why not an older reef? Because the great flood and huge tidal surges 4,400 years ago destroyed all reefs.

# CHAPTER 11

# Fossil Evidence Supports Creation

### Fossil records verify a worldwide flood and young earth.

**Background.** Fossils found in rock strata do not indicate a time period (geological age) when the animals lived. The fossil record vividly shows the sequence of plant and animal death during a worldwide flood that occurred 4,400 years ago. Although we have billions of fossils, we have not one credible fossil showing a transitional (evolutionary) animal changing from one kind of plant or animal into another. If evolution were true, we'd have billions times billions of transitional animal forms from one taxonomic group to another. We have none.

**Fossil Formation.** It is often claimed that fossils take millions of years to form (petrify). Not true. Fossils can form in 20-25 years. There are many examples of fossilized and petrified items that man uses. Fossil records indicate the earth's age is only a few thousand years. The enormous fossil record could only have been created by the extreme cataclysmic death of billions and billions of organisms due to the worldwide flood and the accompanying seismic and tectonic activity.

**No Intermediate Fossils.** Fossils, billions of them, found in various rock layers are similar to currently existing species, or recently extinct plants and animals, including dinosaurs. They are all fully functioning. No transitional forms are found to show evolution from any type of animal to another. No fossils of half fish, half amphibians, or half amphibians to half reptiles, etc., have been found. There is no record where a more complex animal, or a different "kind" of animal evolved from a simpler one. There is no evidence of "partial" systems, such as a human brain, eye, or ear. The fossil records show only complete, fully functioning plants and animals from the very earliest fossils. Commonality between animal species doesn't indicate evolution, it indicates a common designer – God.

**Polystrata Forests.** Polystrata forests are fossilized trees found growing through multiple geologic rock layers. Evolutionists must assume that these trees remained standing for millions of years without falling as sediment and rock formed around them. In reality, a worldwide flood quickly covered these trees with soft sediments, which later hardened, forming the various rock strata (layers) in a matter of days, weeks and months. Many of these trees are upside down, uprooted during the great flood. The Mt. St. Helens eruption caused exactly the same conditions as trees settle and sediment forms around them in Spirit Lake.

Scientists estimate there are 20,000 trees in the bottom of Spirit Lake.

Many of them are buried upright and some are already 15 feet deep in sediments.

These exactly replicate polystrata found in geological layers around the world.

**Graptolite Fossils.** A graptolite is an arthropod. The graptolite fossil is the official New York state fossil. It is also the index fossil evolutionists use to show that a rock layer is 410 million years old. Except, oops! In 1993, living graptolites were found in the South Pacific. Obviously, graptolites could be found in any layer and are not 410 million years old.

**Chlorophyll Still Structured.** In some un-fossilized remains, such as the stomach contents of frozen Woolly Mammoths, magnolia leaves are still green and contain chlorophyll. The chlorophyll would have deteriorated or been absent if these were millions of years old.

**Archeoraptor.** Archeoraptor was heavily promoted by National Geographic Society and Nature magazine as a "feathered dinosaur" and was claimed to be an intermediate evolutionary link between a reptile and a bird. However, it has been shown to be an intentional fraud where two fossils were placed together giving the appearance of a bird's body and a dinosaur's head. Today most scientific organizations continue to ignore evidence of creation, placing this and other fraudulent information on TV "documentaries" and in publications to support their evolutionistic religion, even many years after these items have been proven scientifically false.

# CHAPTER 12

# Radiocarbon Dating Has Limitations

*Radiocarbon dating has limitations and has been misused. It cannot date fossils or rocks and can only date items a few thousand years old, not millions of years old.*

**Background.** Although we've been taught that radiological dating methods are accurate, they are fraught with errors. All radiological data gives extreme age variation, and its interpretation requires many assumptions. Each year scientists keep adding more time to the age of the earth and to rock layers to make things seem more "plausible." A review of science books over the last 20 years shows on average (if you believe the textbooks), the earth is growing older by 28 million years each year. The truth is that new scientific discoveries continue to prove that evolution is a hoax.

**Carbon Dating.** Carbon dating methods aren't accurate and can only measure a few thousand years back in time. If the earth were billions of years old, radioactive carbon (C14) should be virtually absent. However, it's still present today indicating the earth is only a few thousand years old.

**Rocks, Fossils.** Rocks, minerals, and fossils cannot be dated accurately by any known scientific method, including radiometric techniques. Statements that a fossil is millions or billions of years old are merely beliefs or opinions based on very faulty assumptions.

**Rock Age.** A rock aged by two different scientists using the most advanced radiometric technique was reported to be 10,000 years old by one scientist. The other aged the same rock at several million years.

**Living Animals.** Living snails were aged at 27,000 years old by radiometric dating methods. Living penguins have been aged as 20,000 years old. Errors of 1000% or more are common, but the public has been duped into believing radiometric dating is a highly accurate technique.

**Helium.** Nuclear decay creates helium, which is easily lost to the air. The large amount of helium still found in rock layers shows the earth is between 4,000 and 10,000 years old, not billions of years old.

Living snails and penguins have been aged using the most advanced radiometric techniques at 20,000-30,000 years old.

# CHAPTER 13

# Animal Anatomy Supports Creation

### Animal anatomy and function shows a Master Designer, not evolution.

**Background.** Evolutionists attempt to show evolution by using similarities between different groups of animals. These similarities don't show evolution, they show a common designer. Different makes of automobiles have similarities. This doesn't mean one evolved into the other. It shows common design.

**Spontaneous Generation.** Spontaneous generation means that life came from dead or non-living matter. Louis Pasteur disproved this in 1860. However, life from nothing is the main component of macro-evolutionary theory. This belief ignores scientific facts, which show spontaneous generation isn't possible.

**No Intermediates Found.** If one animal type evolved into another type, there should be billions of transitional or intermediate animals and fossils. However, no intermediates, links or crosses have been found. How would an intermediate form survive? Imagine a half reptile, half bird. Also, no intermediate systems, organs or sensory systems have been found, only fully functioning forms remarkably designed for the animal's survival. This shows common design and a common designer. Importantly, if animals evolved, then why aren't the lower, less effective forms, such as fish, continuing to evolve today? Why are no living intermediate forms found? The answer is simple. Evolution didn't happen.

**Natural Selection Loses Genetic Information.** Nowhere can it be shown that an animal gained significant genetic information, organ structure, or sensory capabilities through mutation or natural selection. Natural selection weeds out organisms unfit for survival, but it doesn't cause an animal without a brain to develop one, or change a cat into a dog.

**Vestigial Structures.** Some scientists say that some organs, such as the human tailbone, are vestigial and are not needed, a remnant from man evolving from a lower animal. Actually, in humans, muscles attach to the tailbone that control body functions. It was once said that the human appendix had no function. Today we know the human appendix functions to assist our immune system.

**Whale Appendage Example.** Some bones in whales, man, birds and reptiles show similar structure. Whales have two bones in each flipper, similar to the human arm. Man gave them similar names but that doesn't mean we're related to whales. The similarities show a common designer - God.

**Archaeopteryx.** This fossil is a bird. Evolutionists claimed this was an intermediate between a bird and a reptile because it had beak teeth and claw-like appendages on its wings. Twelve modern species of birds, including the Ibis, common today, have similar claws on their wings. Also, some hummingbirds, have teeth.

**Peppered Moth.** Evolutionists commonly use the Peppered Moth in an attempt to show evolution. This moth has two color variations: light and dark. The dark colored moths survive on dark trees; the light colors survive on light trees. This is not evolution, but shows the greatness of God as our Creator. He made two color varieties to assure survival. Carmakers put heaters and air conditioners in the same car. It shows planning, not evolution.

**Horse Evolution Fraud.** Othniel C. Marsh intentionally falsified horse evolution theory in 1874 when he took horse fossils from around the world and placed them into an order not found in the geological layers. In reality, modern horse fossils are found in the lowest earth strata, below what Marsh termed "ancient" horses. What he called an ancient "horse" is still alive today. Science has proved "horse evolution" to be fully fabricated, but it continues to be found in public school and college textbooks, and in museum displays.

**Haeckel's Embryo Drawings.** These fake drawings supposedly show similarities between different groups of animals in their embryonic stages. However, the drawings are a fraud. The drawings do not resemble actual photos of embryonic development. Haeckel was convicted of fraud by his own university, yet we continue to see his fake drawings in school textbooks more than 100 years later.

## Haeckel's Fake Drawings on Top

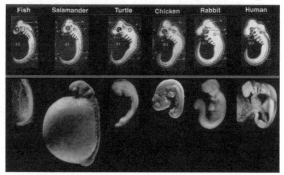

## Actual Embryo Photos on Bottom

**Reptile To Bird.** Evolutionists claim reptiles evolved into birds, however, there are hundreds of differences between reptiles and birds. No credible intermediates between these have been found. The lungs are different. Scales and feathers are different, attach differently, and develop from different genes on the chromosomes. Birds have a 4-chambered heart; reptiles have a 3-chambered heart. Birds have a hard eggshell; reptiles have a leathery eggshell. They have many more differences than similarities, yet evolutionists continue to claim that one group evolved from the other. No evidence supports any evolution or transformation of one type of animal to another.

# Dinosaur & Animal Evidence Supports Creation

*Dinosaurs didn't roam the earth millions of years ago. They lived with man. They were called dragons.*

**Background.** Evolutionists claim that dinosaurs roamed the earth between 30 million and 150 million years ago, before man had "evolved." This is absolutely untrue. Dinosaurs existed in early history since the days of Adam and Eve, but in folklore they were called dragons. Thousands of stories and cave drawings depict actual, recognizable kinds of dinosaurs (called dragons) coexisting with early man. Plus, there are thousands of pieces of current evidence showing that remnant dinosaurs remained in the 19th and 20th centuries. A few smaller specimens may be around today in extremely remote areas of the world.

**Dinosaur Footprints.** In Glenrose, TX, man and dinosaur footprints are found together. The imprints clearly show dinosaur footprints stepping on man's footprint; sometimes the man's footprint is inside the dinosaur footprint.

**Mokela Mbembe.** This is a reported dinosaur, a type of small "brachiosaurus," seen even today by natives and scientists. It continues to be reported in the Congo.

**Pterodactyls.** Pterodactyls have been sighted from numerous places throughout the Congo. The still-surviving species reportedly have a three-foot wingspan; however, in the 20th century, larger specimens were found in several places. You don't hear about these in the media, since these findings are contrary to evolutionary theory.

**Coelacanth.** The coelacanth, a primitive fish, is reported to have lived and become extinct 140 million years ago. Textbooks still show this even though coelacanths have been found alive today.

**Brontosaurus.** The Brontosaurus, still pictured in many youth and school textbooks today, never existed. Archeologists mismatched the head and body of two dinosaurs. What most people think of as a Brontosaurus is actually an Apatosaurus.

## Dinosaur Extinction.

Dinosaurs did not become extinct millions of years ago. There was no earth or dinosaurs millions of years ago. Post-flood earth was totally different than earth in the days of Adam and Eve. The hydrosphere that surrounded earth, was gone. This meant less oxygen and less oxygen pressure. There was more x-ray bombardment and shortened life spans. The climate became varied and inhospitable, including snow and cold. These climatic changes, plus the fact that man hunted dinosaurs, called dragons back then, for sport and food, resulted in the extinction of dinosaurs. Some dinosaur

The brontosaurus, popular in museums and dinosaur literature even today, never existed. Archeologists mis-matched the head and body of two different dinosaurs.

remnants remained into the early 20th century, and there might even be a handful of specimens alive today in remote regions such as the Congo.

# CHAPTER 15

# Human Evidence Supports Creation

*Humankind supports creation and a young earth.*

**Background.** The Bible tells us that the heavens and earth, animals, and mankind were created approximately 6,000 years ago. About 4,400 years ago a worldwide flood killed all mankind and all animals except Noah and his family, and the animals on the ark. This worldwide flood shaped the earth's geological features we see today. Another myth is cavemen. Cavemen didn't exist. Bones found are either ape or man. DNA and other modern identification techniques expose the fraud of "human" evolution.

**Oldest Cultures.** The oldest recorded cultures of man are less than 5,000 years old. Why are there no earlier records? It is because man has only existed for approximately 6,000 years, and early mankind (except Noah and his family) died off in the worldwide flood 4,400 years ago.

**Population Curve.** The human population curve shows man has only existed for about 4,400 years. In 1800, there were one billion people on earth. In 1985, there were 5 billion people on earth. This is nowhere near what you'd expect if man has been on earth for more than a million years as evolutionists claim. Our current population is what you would expect if the population began 4,000 years ago from one family and that each family averaged 2.5 children. If evolution was correct, even if you cut this rate to one fourth, the number of people today would be 1 with 2,100 zeros after it. This is more people than could fit on the total earth surface, and even in our solar system. This alone proves that our population began about 4,000 years ago, at the exact time of the worldwide flood. Also, if evolution were true, there would be billions and billions of people who would have already

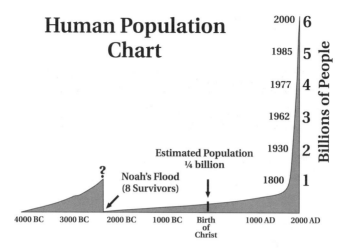

# Human Population Chart

The human population curve shows man only existed for about 4,400 years. If evolution was correct, there would be more persons on earth than could fit on earth or even in our entire solar system. The quantity of dead human remains would make earth and all the planets a human bone pile.

died. Where are all the bones? The human remains would more than completely cover the earth.

**Ancient Cultures.** Many ancient cultures from around the globe have recorded stories and cave drawings depicting a worldwide flood. This flood completely covered the entire earth. Such folklore accounts show remarkable similarities, each to the other, and clearly indicate that the great flood was worldwide.

**Neanderthals.** Many claim Neanderthals were an evolutionary "in-between" – in between ape and man. However, they are obviously human and have a larger brain capacity than man today. It is only our textbook drawings (artistic fabrications) that depict a stooped over "caveman" or "ape-man" looking like half ape, half man, that makes this man appear less man-like and more ape-like.

**Nebraska Man.** Nebraska man, a supposed link between ape and man, was fabricated from a single tooth. A stooped body covered with hair and a primitive face was fabricated to show his closeness in appearance to an ape. Volumes have been written about his physical and mental capabilities. Years later, the tooth was determined to be a pig tooth.

**Piltdown Man.** Piltdown man, a supposed link between ape and man, was a total hoax. An ape jawbone was fitted to a human skull, treated with acid, and this was buried and later "re-discovered." For decades, in magazines, TV and school text-books, Piltdown man was widely reported as the missing link. It was a fraud.

**Lucy.** Lucy is the currently widely publicized missing link for modern man. Here again graphic artists have taken great liber-ties to construct a half human, half apelike being. Archeologists have found a more com-plete skeleton than for other so-called cavemen, however, the skeleton remains incom-plete. Skeletal por-tions that distinc-

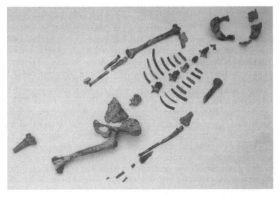

tively separate man from ape, such as the greater portion of the skull, the knee joints, and the ankle and foot bones are missing from Lucy's skeletal finds. Artistic drawings, however, show Lucy with human-like feet and stature, but this is pure conjecture. In reality, Lucy is an ape.

**Unborn Child.** An unborn child forms 15,000 new cells a minute for 9 months. Each cell is more complicated than the space shuttle. Imagine making 15,000 space shuttles a minute. Man can't even begin to imagine the intelligence and awesome creative power of God.

**Human Body and Brain.** The human body has 100 trillion cells. The human brain has 10 billion cells. Each individual cell is more complicated than the most sophisticated computer, and obviously had a designer. We can look at a digital watch and know it had a designer, even if we can't see the designer. In the same manner, the human body and brain, through their intri-cate design, show mankind had a designer more intelligent than we can even imagine.

# Life After Death

*"... Eye hath not seen, nor ear heard, neither have entered into the heart of man, the things that God has prepared for them that love him"* (1 Corinthians 2:9).

# CHAPTER 16

# Life After Death

**God gave sinful man
a way to save himself through
His Son, Jesus Christ.**

Harry Truman (not the former president) lived at the base of Mt. St. Helens on Spirit Lake. Seismologists predicted the 1980 eruption was coming and evacuated most people from the immediate area. Harry Truman, however, refused to leave. He didn't heed repeated warnings of the 1980 Mt. St. Helen's eruption. Harry Truman is still there – buried under tons of ash and debris.

Similarly, mankind has heard the story of Jesus Christ, and most have failed to believe.

After a short life on earth, we all pass on. The good news is that God has guaranteed us eternal life in heaven if we trust and believe in His Son, Jesus Christ. However, many fail to heed this message. God tells us that some day there will be a new heaven and a new earth. This new heaven and new earth will be wonderful, beyond what the human mind can even imagine: "... *Eye hath not seen, nor ear heard, neither have entered into the heart of man, the things which God hath prepared for them that love him*" (1 Corinthians 2:9).

## We Must Ask for God's Gift of Eternal Life

To receive eternal life in God's new heaven we must believe in His

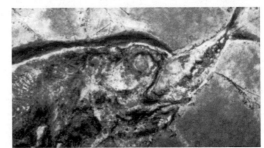

Neither of these fish expected to die. Yet they died quickly and unexpectedly.

Son, Jesus Christ. About 2,000 years ago Jesus Christ was born as the Son of God taking on human flesh. He was crucified on the cross, but three days later arose from the dead. He sacrificed Himself for us.

In the Bible, Romans 3:23 tells us that we all are sinners: *"For all have sinned and come short of the glory of God."* Romans 6:23 tells us that the penalty for sin is eternal death in hell: *"the wages of sin is death."*

Happily, however, Romans 6:23 also says that since Jesus died for our sins, we can receive God's gift of eternal life in heaven: *"but the gift of God is eternal life through Jesus Christ our Lord."*

To receive eternal life in heaven we need to repent of our sins and ask Jesus to come into our lives: *"For whosoever shall call upon the name of the Lord shall be saved"* (Romans 10:13). Or, stated another way, *"For God so loved the world that he gave his only begotten Son, that whosoever believeth in him shall not perish but have everlasting life"* (John 3:16).

If you are not saved, simply pray and repent of your sins, asking Jesus to come into your life. The words you pray aren't important, but you must believe the words in your heart.

## Example Salvation Prayer

*"Dear Jesus, I know I'm a sinner, and I deserve to die for my sins. I know you died on the cross to save me from my sins. I repent my sins and make you my Lord and Master. Please save me and guide my life from this moment on. Amen."*

Once you've received Jesus into your life, you have become a child of God and are guaranteed eternal life in heaven. The next step is to grow spiritually by joining a Bible-believing church, reading the Bible, praying, and fellowshipping with other Christians.

# CHAPTER 17

# What Can God-Believing People Do?

Sad, but true, our society has been brainwashed by a false belief in evolution. Here are a few ways you can protect future generations and help expose evolution for the hoax it is.

### Give Kids Correct Information.
Feed your kids correct information. To provide an overview, buy this book for your school library, public libraries, schoolteachers, friends, neighbor's kids and others, and distribute it to students and young people in your local schools and youth organizations. This book is available for purchase at www.creationproof.com. Discounts are offered for quantity purchases.

### Public Schools.
Donate creation materials (books, tapes, DVD's, this book) to public and school libraries. See reference page for sources.

### Correct School Textbooks.
Petition to have school textbooks corrected and known scientific errors removed. Add creation and intelligent design evidence to school science books. Most states have accuracy laws. Evolution information can be proven wrong. Meet with educators and school officials to complain about evolution (a religion) being taught in public schools. Put warning labels on public school textbooks that the book contains inaccurate materials.

**Textbook Selection Committee.** Get on the local school-book selection committee. Select the best of the worst textbooks, those that contain the least amount of evolution. Then, write the publisher and tell them why you chose their book. Write to the other publishers and tell them why you did not select their book.

**Christian Schooling.** If possible, get your kids out of public school, and into a Bible-based Christian school that teaches biblical creation.

**Study the Bible.** Have your youngsters read and study the Bible. Teach them the biblical story of creation. Explain the difference between evolution and creation and how science backs creation.

**Do Not Support the NEA.** Teachers, do not support the National Education Association (NEA). It has taken antagonistic stands against creation, the Bible and God.

**Support Creation Ministries.** Support creation science ministries to help spread the truth about creation and evolution. Our ministry and most others are funded by your contributions.

**Dinosaur Ministry.** Start a pre-school dinosaur workshop and use this to tell youngsters about the true age of the earth, dinosaurs and how the earth was created.

**Volunteer.** Volunteer to give creation-based tours at your local museum or historical exhibit. Work to remove false materials from your local museums and geological exhibits and to add creation exhibits. Give support to one of the creation museums. See reference section.

**Prayer.** Start a prayer campaign. Be a prayer warrior.

For additional information on creation and evolution, or to learn more on how you can help, visit www.creationproof.com, or contact Creation Science Network, 4607 NE Cedar Creek Rd., Woodland, WA 98674. Email us at omni@creationproof.com.

# ORGANIZATIONS

**Institute for Creation Research.** P.O. Box 2667, El Cajon, CA 92021, www.icr.org. Offers a wealth of technical scientific information and scientific research findings on all areas of evolution and creation, including Acts & Facts, Days of Praise and News and Updates.

**Creation Science Evangelism.** 29 Cummings Rd., Pensacola, FL 32503, www.drdino.com and www.dinosauradventureland.com. Offers full information on creation science for all ages, particularly youngsters. Has a creation science museum at Dinosaur Adventure Land that includes a science center, creation museum and theme park.

**Creation Moments.** P.O. Box 839, Foley, MN 56329, www.creationmoments.org. Provides daily email newsletters and offers a broad array of creation science materials, facts and research materials.

**Answers In Genesis.** P.O. Box 6330, Florence, KY 41022, www.answersingenesis.org. Offers books and other educational materials, including a variety of scientific reference materials. Has a creation science museum located near Cincinnati International Airport in northern Kentucky.

**Creation Evidence Museum.** P.O. Box 309, Glen Rose, TX 76043, www.creationevidence.org. Offers books and other materials including a creation science museum containing a variety of displays and a great assortment of archeological dig artifacts.

**Seven Wonders Museum.** Mount St. Helens Creation Information Center. 4749 Spirit Lake Highway, Silverlake, WA 98645, www.creationism.org/sthelens/. Offers museum displays, bookstore, field trips and creation information on Mt. St. Helens.

**Creation Science Network.** 4607 NE Cedar Creek Rd., Woodland, WA 98674, www.creationproof.com. Offers books and other materials and links to other top creation web sites.

# BOOKS

*Are You Being Brainwashed? Propaganda in Science Textbooks.* Dr. Kent Hovind, Creation Science Evangelism, www.drdino.com.

*Creation Facts of Life.* Dr. Gary Parker, Master Books, 1994, www.newleafpress.net.

*Why Do Men Believe Evolution Against All Odds.* Dr. Carl E. Baugh, Hearthstone Publishing, 1999, www.creationevidence.org.

*The Revised and Expanded Answers Book. The 20 Most-Asked Questions About Creation, Evolution, and the Book of Genesis, Answered!* Don Batten Editor, Dr. Ken Ham et. al., Master Books, 1990, www.masterbooks.net.

*I Don't Have Enough Faith To Be An Atheist.* Norman Geisler & Frank Turek, Crossway Books, 2004, www.crossway.com.

*Unlocking the Mysteries of Creation.* Dr. Dennis R. Petersen, Master Books, 2002, www.masterbooks.net.

*The Lie: Evolution.* Dr. Ken Ham, Master Books, 1987, www.masterbooks.net.

*The Young Earth.* Dr. John D. Morris, Master Books, 1994, www.masterbooks.net

*Teaching Science in Public Schools.* Dr. Duane T. Gish, Institute for Creation Research, 1995, www.icr.org.

*Noah's Ark: A Feasibility Study.* John Woodmorappe, Institute for Creation Research, 1996, www.icr.org.